Contents

1. We Are Made in God's Image — 9

God's Word: Psalm 139:1–2, 13–14; Genesis 2:7–8, 18, 21–23

Catholic Signs & Symbols: The Church

Meet Jesus: Second Person of the Trinity

Rite Focus: The Perfect Image of God

My Family in Our Parish

2. We Live in Covenant with God — 19

God's Word: Matthew 9:10–13; Joel 2:13

Catholic Signs & Symbols: Baptismal Water

Meet Jesus: The Savior

Rite Focus: God Keeps His Promises

My Family in Our Parish

3. We Are Called to Forgiveness — 29

God's Word: Psalm 86:4b–6; Luke 15:11–24a

Catholic Signs & Symbols: Confessional or Reconciliation Room

Meet Jesus: The Healer

Rite Focus: Our Conscience Helps Guide Us

My Family in Our Parish

4. We Come to Reconciliation — 39

God's Word: John 15:9–14; John 10:3–5, 11–15

Catholic Signs & Symbols: Stoles

Meet Jesus: The Good Shepherd

Rite Focus: The Rite of Penance

My Family in Our Parish

5. We Confess & Do Penance — 49

God's Word: John 14:23–26; Luke 19:2–10

Catholic Signs & Symbols: Hands

Meet Jesus: Christ the King

Rite Focus: Confession and Penance— The Heart of Reconciliation

My Family in Our Parish

6. We Are Forgiven & We Forgive — 59

God's Word: John 20:20b–23; Matthew 18:20–22

Catholic Signs & Symbols: The Sign of the Cross

Meet Jesus: Jesus and His Body, the Church

Rite Focus: God Forgives Us

My Family in Our Parish

The Subcommittee on the Catechism, United States Conference of Catholic Bishops, has found this catechetical text, copyright 2016, to be in conformity with the *Catechism of the Catholic Church*.

Nihil Obstat
Father Jeremiah Payne, Censor Librorum, Diocese of Orlando

Imprimatur
✠ Most Rev. John Noonan
Bishop of Orlando
January 19, 2016

Our Sunday Visitor Curriculum Division
200 Noll Plaza, Huntington, IN 46750
1-800-348-2440

See acknowledgments on page 88.

Encounter with Christ: Reconciliation Child Book
ISBN: 978-1-61278-462-5
Item Number: CU5421
4 5 6 7 8 9 015016 22 21 20 19 18
Webcrafters, Inc., Madison, WI, USA;
May 2018; Job# 136095

In this Book

The Sacrament of Penance and Reconciliation is a precious gift to us from God. This book will help you prepare to receive this gift. There are many features in this book that will help you to learn how Jesus offers us his love and help through this Sacrament.

Meet Jesus

Learn more about each of these titles of Jesus.

Page 11: Second Person of the Trinity
Page 21: The Savior
Page 31: The Healer
Page 41: The Good Shepherd
Page 51: Christ the King
Page 61: Jesus and His Body, the Church

Circle any ways you have heard someone talk about Jesus.

Catholic Signs & Symbols

Many signs and symbols connect us to the Sacrament of Penance and Reconciliation.

Page 11: The Church
Page 21: Baptismal Water
Page 31: Confessional or Reconciliation Room
Page 41: Stoles
Page 51: Hands
Page 61: The Sign of the Cross

Have you seen any of these signs or symbols in your parish church? Draw a star next to the ones you have seen.

God's Word

Your book includes stories, Psalms, and teachings from the Bible. You'll learn more about being a follower of Jesus and a member of the Church.

• The All-knowing and Ever-present God; The Creation of Man and Woman
• The Call of Matthew; Gracious and Merciful
• Prayer in Time of Distress; The Parable of the Lost Son
• The Vine and the Branches; The Good Shepherd
• The Advocate; Zacchaeus the Tax Collector
• Appearance to the Disciples; How Often Must We Forgive?

Which of these stories or sayings from the Bible have you heard before? Do you have a favorite? Put a check mark next to it.

CATHOLIC FAITH WORDS

Which of these important words or phrases have you heard?
Place a check mark next to one or two. Then tell a partner or
family member what each means!

- [ ] Beatitudes
- [ ] Body of Christ
- [ ] Church
- [ ] confession
- [ ] conscience
- [ ] contrition
- [ ] conversion
- [ ] covenant
- [ ] free will
- [ ] grace
- [ ] Holy Trinity
- [ ] Kingdom of God
- [ ] mercy
- [ ] mortal sin

- [ ] mystery
- [ ] Original Sin
- [ ] Paschal Mystery
- [ ] penance
- [ ] Prayer of Absolution
- [ ] reconcile
- [ ] Seven Sacraments
- [ ] sin
- [ ] temptation
- [ ] Ten Commandments
- [ ] venial sin
- [ ] Works of Mercy

Our Parish

Write the name of your parish below.

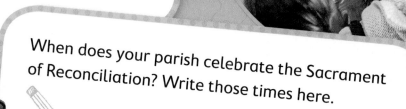

When does your parish celebrate the Sacrament of Reconciliation? Write those times here.

Where in your parish does this Sacrament take place? If you don't know, ask your pastor, your catechist, or a family member. Draw this place in the space below or take a picture of it and paste it here.

Who are some of the people helping you prepare to receive your First Penance? Fill in their names below.

My catechist:

My pastor:

Name some ways that your parish brings healing and peace to your local community. Ask your pastor, your catechist, or a family member for ideas!

MY FAMILY

Your family is an important part of your faith journey, too! In fact, the family is called the "domestic Church" because it's the first place you learn about our Catholic faith and how to live as Jesus asks. You learn how to say and show you are sorry. You experience forgiveness. You forgive others.

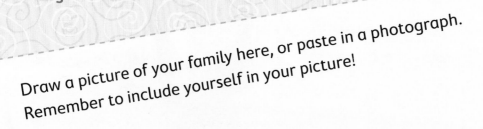

Draw a picture of your family here, or paste in a photograph. Remember to include yourself in your picture!

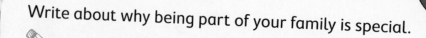

Write about why being part of your family is special.

When do you feel close to your family? List special times that you share.

Write about one responsibility that you have in your family.

What is one family rule that you have? Explain how this rule helps you to know how to treat one another.

Disciples Sharing *Name one way your family shows love to each other. Talk about ways your family shows forgiveness to one another.*

About Me

Fill in the boxes with information about you.

What I like to think about:

What I like to talk about:

What I keep close to my heart:

What I like to use my hands for:

Where I like to go:

Disciples Sharing
How do you know that God loves you? How can you share this love with others?

As you work through these sessions, you will learn more about God's love and mercy. You will also learn more about yourself.

So, let's begin!

1 We Are Made in God's Image

♡ Let Us Pray

Leader: Heavenly Father, we thank you for the gift of our lives. Thank you for making us your children. Thank you for the gift of your Son, who died and rose for us. Thank you, also, for the gift of the Holy Spirit, who dwells in our hearts.

All: Make us a sign of your love for all to see. Amen.

God's Word

LORD,...you know me:
> you know when I sit and stand;
> you understand my thoughts ...
> you knit me in my mother's womb.
I praise you, because I am wonderfully made;
> wonderful are your works!
My very self you know. **Psalm 139:1–2, 13–14**

> What did you hear God say to you today?

Opening Video
sacraments.osv.com

9

Things I Make

Isn't it fun to make something with your hands? You can watch your ideas come to life!

When you want to make something, you have to think about what you want it to be and what you want it to do. You need to think about its purpose. You may make more than one thing. When you create something, it may have many pieces that work together.

Think about something that would be super fun to make. Draw your creation.

Catholic Signs & Symbols

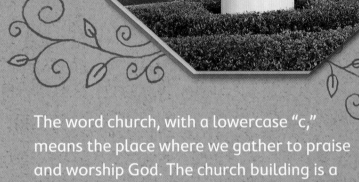

THE CHURCH God is *our* Creator. He made us to be in relationship with him and others. He wants us to be in communion. This means to be together in love.

God calls all people to belong to his Church through faith in Jesus Christ. We become part of God's Church at Baptism.

The word **Church**, with a capital "C," means the community of baptized people who believe in God and follow Jesus, the Son of God. The Church is a sign of our communion with God and each other.

The word church, with a lowercase "c," means the place where we gather to praise and worship God. The church building is a sign of the Church, God's family.

Meet Jesus

SECOND PERSON OF THE TRINITY The **Holy Trinity** is the one God in three Divine Persons—God the Father, God the Son, and God the Holy Spirit. The three Persons of the Trinity are a relationship of perfect love. We are invited into this relationship.

God the Father loves us so much that he sent his Son, Jesus, to us. Jesus tells us, "whoever has seen me has seen the Father" (**John 14:9**). In Jesus, we see God's invitation to know and love him. And the Holy Spirit helps us to respond to Jesus' invitation.

Created by God

God created each and every one of us. We are made in God's image and likeness, male and female. He has a purpose for each of us. Our hearts are filled with thankfulness and joy because we belong to God!

God's Word

The Creation of Man and Woman Then the LORD God formed the man out of the dust of the ground and blew into his nostrils the breath of life, and the man became a living being. The LORD God planted a garden in Eden, in the east, and placed there the man whom he had formed.... The LORD God said: It is not good for the man to be alone. I will make a helper suited to him....

So the LORD God cast a deep sleep on the man, and while he was asleep, he took out one of his ribs and closed up its place with flesh. The LORD God then built the rib that he had taken from the man into a woman. When he brought her to the man, the man said: "This one, at last, is bone of my bones and flesh of my flesh; This one shall be called 'woman,' for out of man this one has been taken." Genesis 2:7–8, 18, 21–23

Made for God and Each Other

This reading is from Genesis, the first book of the Bible. This book teaches us that God is the Creator of heaven and Earth. It also tells us that everything God creates is good. We learn that human beings are different from all the rest of creation. We are made in God's image and likeness. God created us to be in relationship with others and all the wonders of creation.

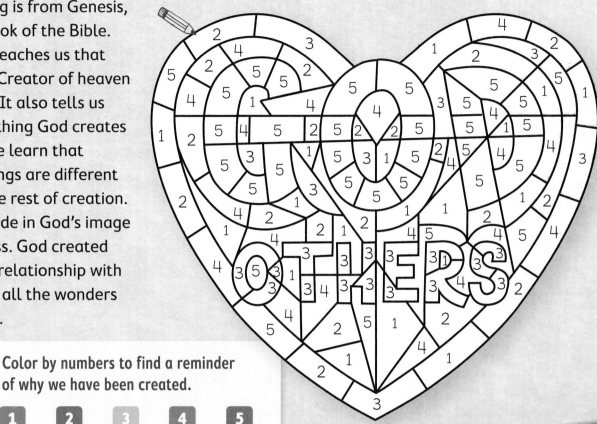

Color by numbers to find a reminder of why we have been created.

1   2   3   4   5

Entering the Mystery

A **mystery** is a truth about God that can't be known unless God makes it known to us. A mystery is difficult to understand with our mind or our senses. But we can begin to understand it through faith and signs. God makes this possible because of his love for us.

God created us out of love. We are free to choose to love him back. Sometimes we choose actions that do not show love. But God doesn't stop loving us, no matter what we do. When you participate in the Sacrament of Penance and Reconciliation, you will experience the power of God's forgiveness and love.

The Perfect Image of God

We are all created in the image and likeness of God. However, Jesus is the most perfect image of God. This is because he *is* God. He was sent to save us and to teach us. Jesus is God and man. Jesus is fully divine. He is also fully human. He is just like us in every way, except that he never sinned. God the Father sent Jesus, his Son, to show us his love. He was sent to teach us how to live as God's children.

Look at the pictures on this page and the next. We see Jesus showing his Father's love. Discuss each picture. Write words that describe Jesus' actions.

Seeing God in Others

What does being made in God's image mean? It does not mean we look like God. It does mean that each human being was created to live like God. This includes you, your parents, your family, your friends, and people you don't know! God created all of us to love and give of ourselves. Anything that is good is from God and points to him.

> 💬 **Disciples Sharing** *Think of someone you love. Talk about why you love that person. What makes this person special? The kind and loving things this person does makes his or her light shine. You can see God in that person!*

Free to Choose

Being made in God's image also means we are given **free will**. This is the God-given freedom to make choices. We are given the ability to obey God and to do good. We are free to be in communion with him. But we are also free to choose otherwise.

We may choose to let our light shine, as Jesus did. Or we could choose to hide it. When we choose to disobey God on purpose and do what we know is wrong, we **sin**. We use God's gift of free will to choose against his love.

As we prepare for the Sacrament of Penance and Reconciliation, we will learn how sin changes things. Sin changes our relationships, the world, and us. Thankfully, God's love does not change. He has made a never-ending promise to be with us.

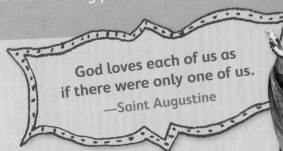

God loves each of us as if there were only one of us.
—Saint Augustine

Games & Downloads

Special Blessings

A blessing is a prayer. It calls God's power and care upon a person, place, thing, or task. A blessing shows that we understand that God is our Creator and we need him.

God creates all people and blesses them. We often ask God to bless others for special reasons. Blessings can be for people you know personally. They can also be for people you know about.

A prayer of blessings is just one type of prayer.

➡ *For other types of prayers, turn to page 82.*

Parents bless their children by marking them with the Sign of the Cross.

✏ **On the first line, write the name of someone who needs a special blessing. Then write what he or she needs.**

Dear God, please bless ------------------------------------

with ------------------------------------

💬 **Disciples Sharing** *Have you ever had something blessed? What was it?*

16

Respect God's Image

It is not always easy to see the image of God in each other. We may only see what we do not like in someone else.

Think about someone you find difficult to get along with. Maybe it's someone who has been unkind to you. But, you can see God's image in this person, too.

Be sure to keep this person in your prayers tonight. Ask for Jesus' help. He can help you treat this person as he would.

Write one way in which God shines in a person you do not get along with.

Write one thing you can do to be kind to that person.

Pray the closing prayer.

My Family in Our Parish

We Are Made in God's Image

The Church Building Before or after Mass, look closely at the windows, statues, and art in your church. They are meant to inspire your mind and heart to think about God. They can help you enter into the mystery of God. What in your church inspires you to connect to God?

Draw a picture of something in your church that inspires you. Or take a picture of it and paste it below.

 Disciples Sharing Each person in your family was made in God's image. This can be especially hard to remember when you aren't getting along. What are some ways to show you are thankful for each member of your family?

Session videos, games, multimedia glossary, Sunday readings and backgrounds, Sacrament FAQs, reflections, and more at **sacraments.osv.com**

2 We Live in Covenant with God

 Let Us Pray

Leader: God, you are kind and merciful. Send your Holy Spirit to help us grow closer to you. Give us the desire to show others your love every day.

All: We pray that you hear us, O Lord. Amen.

God's Word

Many tax collectors and sinners came and sat with Jesus and his disciples. The Pharisees saw this and said to his disciples, "Why does your teacher eat with tax collectors and sinners?" He heard this and said, "Those who are well do not need a physician, but the sick do.... I did not come to call the righteous but sinners." Matthew 9:10–13

What did you hear God say to you today?

 Opening Video
sacraments.osv.com

Promises

A promise is a commitment or pledge to do something. We make promises to other people. We can make promises to ourselves, too. We can even make promises to God.

✏️ **Think about a time you kept a promise that you made. Write about it in the spaces below.**

I made a promise to _____

that I would _____

_____.

How did you keep your promise? Act out, draw, write about, or tell about what you did.

✏️

Disciples Sharing *Talk about why it is important to keep a promise.*

Catholic Signs & Symbols

BAPTISMAL WATER Baptismal water is a powerful sign of God's grace and love. It is a sign of Jesus' promise of new life in him. At our Baptism, our parents make a special promise. They promise that they will help us grow as a disciple of Jesus. They make this promise to God. They also make this promise to the Church.

The priest or deacon pours holy water over our head three times. He says, "I baptize you in the name of the Father, and of the Son, and of the Holy Spirit." By the power of the Holy Spirit, we become one with Jesus.

Water has many purposes. We need it to live. It cleans us. It is life-giving and powerful. In Baptism, water is not just a sign of new life. It gives us new life in Christ. It is a symbol of the grace that God gives us in this Sacrament.

Sprinkling Rite

Meet Jesus

THE SAVIOR At our Baptism, our parents are asked, "What name do you give your child?" Names often have special meaning. Jesus' name has a very special meaning. In the language Mary and Joseph spoke, *Jesus* means "God helps" or "God saves." This is the perfect name for Jesus. God the Father sent Jesus to save us from sin and death. What a gift Jesus is to us. We are so loved by God!

Made for Love

Jesus is our Savior. But why do we need to be saved? God created us out of love. He shared his life with us. God gave our first parents all that they needed. They had happiness and love with God. They lived in harmony with each other.

But our first parents chose to disobey God. They turned away from his love. They did not trust in his care for them. They put themselves before God.

This disobedience is called Original Sin. **Original Sin** is the first sin that was committed by Adam and Eve. Since then, sin has been present throughout the world. Original Sin affects every person.

Even though Adam and Eve sinned, God never stopped loving them. And he never stops loving us. His love never changes. God is faithful no matter what we say or do.

God's Word

Gracious and Merciful Rend your hearts, not your garments,
        and return to the Lord, your God,
For he is gracious and merciful,
        slow to anger, abounding in
        steadfast love.... Joel 2:13

When Humans Fail, God Still Loves

When Adam and Eve chose to act against God's will, life changed. The harmony between God and humans was lost. Suffering, death, and the tendency to sin entered our world. We are all born with Original Sin. We are tempted to do wrong.

But, we are still free to choose to live in right relationship with God and others. We are still responsible for our choices and their consequences.

God wants the very best for us. The very best is God. So God the Father sent his Son, Jesus, to live among us. Jesus shows us how much the Father loves us. God's love is so great that he gave his Son's life for our sins. Jesus is our Savior who heals our relationship with God.

 Color the picture that shows an act of love. Discuss how love is being shown.

Entering the Mystery

Because of the **Paschal Mystery**, we have the chance to live forever with God. The Paschal Mystery is the suffering, Death, Resurrection, and Ascension of Jesus. Our relationship with God is healed through Jesus' gift of himself.

In Baptism, the Holy Spirit unites us to Jesus. We die to our old lives and rise to a new life in Jesus. We enter into Jesus' Paschal Mystery.

God Keeps His Promises

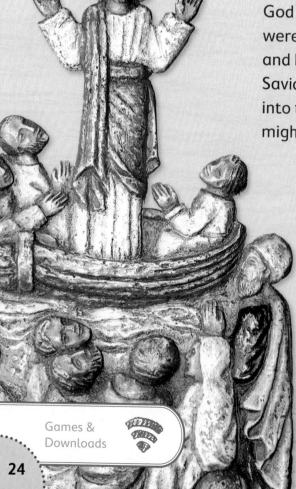

Original Sin damaged man and woman's relationship with God. Their relationship with each other and the world was also damaged.

The Good News is that God will never turn away from us. The Old Testament is filled with stories of God's goodness. We can read about his saving mercy. **Mercy** is kindness and concern shown to those who have wronged us or are suffering. God makes a **covenant**, or sacred promise, with the people of Israel. God promises them that they will be his People. And he will be their God.

God sent the prophets to remind his People that they were not living as they should. But they continued to sin and break the covenant. So God promised to send them a Savior. Saint John tells us, "For God did not send his Son into the world to condemn the world, but that the world might be saved through him" (**John 3:17**).

In Jesus, we are given a new covenant. When we are baptized, we become one with Jesus. We receive God's grace. He takes from us Original Sin and any personal sins. We are forgiven and born into a new life of grace. This **grace** is a share in God's life and help. We become sisters and brothers of Christ.

Games & Downloads

Personal Sin and Grace

Because he is both God and man, Jesus gave us back the possibility of a life in friendship with God. But as humans, we have free will. We may choose to turn away from God's love and to sin. We may disobey him on purpose by doing what we know is wrong. The new life of grace from Baptism can be weakened or even lost by sin. We may find ourselves wanting to do something we should not, or not wanting to do something we should. This is called **temptation**.

Thankfully, God constantly loves us. He calls us back from sin and temptation to life with him. He wants us to remain in communion with him. Through the Holy Spirit and his presence in the Church, we have many opportunities to receive grace. We can receive this grace most especially through the **Seven Sacraments**. These are special signs and celebrations that Jesus gave his Church. They allow us to share in God's life and work.

Baptism, Eucharist, and Penance have a special connection. These Sacraments **reconcile** us to God and one another. They restore our relationships with God and others. We are separated from God by sin. But we are reunited with God and others through these Sacraments. ➡ *Go to page 69 to learn more about the Seven Sacraments.*

Forgiveness

After Baptism, God offers his mercy and forgiveness of sins in a special Sacrament of forgiveness. The Church calls this Sacrament by different names: the Sacrament of Conversion, Confession, Penance, or Reconciliation. Sometimes it's called the Sacrament of Penance and Reconciliation.

In the empty labels, write the name of the Sacrament being celebrated.

Friendships Are Important

Sadly there is sin in the world. However, we know that this world is still good. God's image in us can never be taken away. This is true even when our actions don't reflect God's image as strongly as they could. But Jesus shows us how to be faithful to the Father. He shows us how to be a true child of God. He teaches us how to act with love toward others.

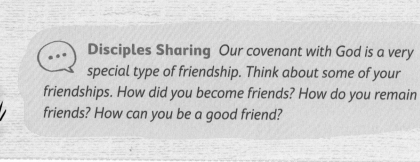

Disciples Sharing *Our covenant with God is a very special type of friendship. Think about some of your friendships. How did you become friends? How do you remain friends? How can you be a good friend?*

Find pictures that represent friendship and paste them here. Tell why you chose these pictures. What do they show us about friendship?

Paste here

Paste here

Life in the New Covenant

Jesus makes it possible for human beings to have again what God created us to have. He wants us to live forever in oneness with him. To receive that gift, we must have a strong connection to Jesus. Our connection is strengthened as we prepare for and celebrate the Sacrament of Reconciliation.

Look at the friendship bracelet below. The individual cords braided together make a stronger, single cord.

What can you do to be a good friend to Jesus? What are some ways you can make your connection to Jesus stronger? Write three ways below.

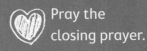
Pray the closing prayer.

My Family *in* Our Parish

We Live in Covenant with God

Holy Water Fonts Before Mass begins, go inside your church. Find all of the holy water fonts. This is where holy water is kept.

Draw the inside of your church. Mark where the fonts are located.

You might notice that the holy water fonts are all located near something similar. Why do you think that is?

Next, mark where the baptismal font (the place where people are baptized) is in your diagram.

 Disciples Sharing After Mass, ask the priest for some holy water to take home. Or ask the parish staff if there are any holy water bottles you may have. As a family, discuss a special place you could keep the holy water. What are some times you could bless yourselves?

Session videos, games, multimedia glossary, Sunday readings and backgrounds, Sacrament FAQs, reflections, and more at **sacraments.osv.com**

3 We Are Called to Forgiveness

 ## Let Us Pray

Leader: Father, your love for us has no limits. You sent your Son, Jesus, to help us grow closer to you and teach us how to live. Let your Spirit guide us each day.

All: Fill our hearts with faith, our days with good works, and our lives with your love. Amen.

God's Word

To you, Lord, I lift up my soul.
Lord, you are good and forgiving,
    most merciful to all who call on you.
LORD, hear my prayer.... Psalm 86:4b–6

What did you hear God say to you today?

 Opening Video
sacraments.osv.com

29

Making Changes

Sometimes our behaviors don't show love. Maybe we were being rude or unkind. Maybe we weren't listening when our parents spoke to us. We may have ignored our chores. Our teachers or parents may have had to correct us many times!

Sometimes we just don't want to change. We may make excuses or blame someone else.

Our bad habits can make it hard to have friends or be healthy. They can also hurt our relationship with God.

💬 **Disciples Sharing** *Think about a habit you have had that didn't show love or respect. How did you know that you needed to change?*

Who has helped you learn behaviors and habits that show love and respect for God, others, and yourself?

Catholic Signs & Symbols

CONFESSIONAL OR RECONCILIATION ROOM

We need the Holy Spirit's help to change what keeps us from loving God. We receive that help in a special way through the Sacrament of Penance. We often celebrate the Sacrament of Penance in a confessional or in a Reconciliation room.

In these spaces, the priest waits for people to come. The people come to confess their sins and receive God's forgiveness. Entering the confessional or Reconciliation room is a sign of our willingness to change. We know that God's forgiveness and healing is waiting for us. This should bring us joy and make us smile.

Meet Jesus

THE HEALER The Gospels tell us that "Jesus went around to all the towns and villages ... curing every disease and illness" (**Matthew 9:35**). Jesus cured people who could not see or walk. Jesus didn't use medicines to heal. He healed by his divine power as the Son of God.

Jesus also healed people's hearts. He prayed with them when they were worried. He stayed with them when they were afraid. Jesus forgave them when their hearts were sad because of something they had done. Jesus healed people's bodies and souls.

More Than We Can Imagine

Many people who came to Jesus needed to make changes. Jesus saw that these people needed healing. He knew they would find healing in God. He told the story below to help them understand how deeply God loves and forgives us.

God's Word

The Parable of the Lost Son

Then he said, "A man had two sons, and the younger son said to his father, 'Father, give me the share of your estate that should come to me.' So the father divided the property between them.

After a few days, the younger son collected all his belongings and set off to a distant country where he squandered his inheritance.... When he had freely spent everything, a severe famine struck that country.... So he hired himself out to one of the local citizens who sent him to his farm to tend the swine. And he longed to eat his fill of the pods on which the swine fed, but nobody gave him any. Coming to his senses he thought, 'How many of my father's hired workers have more than enough food to eat, but here am I, dying from hunger. I shall get up and go to my father ...'"

So he got up and went back to his father. While he was still a long way off, his father caught sight of him, and was filled with compassion. He ran to his son, embraced him and kissed him. His son said to him, 'Father, I have sinned against heaven and against you; I no longer deserve to be called your son.' But his father ordered his servants, 'Quickly bring the finest robe and put it on him; put a ring on his finger and sandals on his feet.... Then let us celebrate with a feast, because this son of mine was dead, and has come to life again; he was lost, and has been found.'" Luke 15:11—24a

Always Waiting to Forgive

Jesus told this parable to a group of people who felt lost. He knew they needed to hear about God's love and forgiveness. Jesus understood that they needed healing.

God's love is like the father's love in the parable. God doesn't just wait for us to come to him. He runs to meet us! God sent his own Son to show us the way back to him.

God's love does not change. We don't do anything to earn his love or his forgiveness. The Holy Spirit helps us see and accept the consequences of our actions. He will lead us back to the Father who always loves us.

Help the lost son find his way home to his father.

start

finish

Entering the Mystery

God is happy when we admit the things we've done wrong and respond to his love. He is happy when we have a change of heart. The Parable of the Lost Son helps us to understand this. If we are sorry, God's forgiving love will always welcome us home. God's love is so great that it is hard to imagine. The Sacrament of Reconciliation helps us to begin to know how great his love for us is.

God's Laws Teach Us

We make choices every day. Some choices are more important than others. What helps us to make good and loving choices?

When God gave the **Ten Commandments** to Moses, he gave all of us laws to help us. They help us to know how to love God and others. By following these Commandments, we learn how to live the right way. We learn to live God's way! We grow closer to God and to others.

★ The first three Commandments show us how to love God. They tell us how to be in right relationship with him. They guide us to honor and serve God.

★ The other seven Commandments teach us how to love our neighbors. They tell us how to live in right relationship with those around us.

Go to page 76 for a list of the Ten Commandments. In each box below, write the number of one Commandment. Then name one specific thing you can do, or not do, to follow that Commandment.

LOVE OF GOD
COMMANDMENTS ONE TO THREE

Commandment

I can live it this week by

LOVE OF NEIGHBOR
COMMANDMENTS FOUR TO TEN

Commandment

I can live it this week by

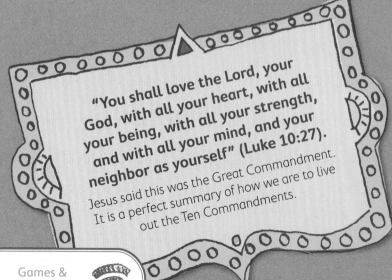

"You shall love the Lord, your God, with all your heart, with all your being, with all your strength, and with all your mind, and your neighbor as yourself" (Luke 10:27). Jesus said this was the Great Commandment. It is a perfect summary of how we are to live out the Ten Commandments.

Games & Downloads

Disciples Sharing *How do you show Jesus' love to others in the choices that you make?*

Help in Making Choices

God wants us to make the right decision about important choices. Jesus teaches us how to make choices that show love. In the **Beatitudes**, Jesus shows us the way to true happiness. He tells us how to live in God's Kingdom now and always. → *Go to page 77 for more on the Beatitudes.*

And in his New Commandment, Jesus tells us that we should love one another as he has loved us.

As disciples of Jesus, we know how much God loves us. We return God's love by obeying his laws and doing his will. He gave us the gift of our conscience. Our **conscience** is an ability given to us by God that helps us make choices about right and wrong.

We have to know God's laws so our conscience can help us make good decisions. We must form our conscience.

Many people help us to learn right from wrong. This includes parents, families, teachers, priests, and loved ones.

The Bible guides us and tells us how to live in God's friendship. The Church and our loved ones help us to understand God's Word in the Bible.

The Church teaches us how to make choices based on Jesus' teachings.

And we trust that God draws us to what is good through the guidance of the Holy Spirit.

35

Examining My Conscience

☐ Have I been respectful to my parents and God today?

☐ How many pieces of candy can I have?

☐ Have I been helpful today?

☐ Have I brushed my teeth today?

Put a check mark by the questions you think would be important to ask yourself as you examine your conscience.

Thank You GOD

☐ Have I thanked God today?

☐ What is my favorite color?

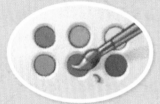

☐ How have I treated my friends today?

☐ Have I prayed today?

So how can we prepare to celebrate the Sacrament of Penance and Reconciliation? First, we can pray! We can ask God to send his Holy Spirit to us. He will help us to get ready and to examine our conscience. We can ask ourselves, "How well have I followed the Ten Commandments, the Great Commandment, and the Beatitudes?" ➡ *You can find examples of an examination of conscience on pages 80–81.*

We should examine our conscience every day. There are questions we can ask ourselves to do this examination of conscience. Examining our conscience helps us to change our attitudes and actions. It helps us to see where we really need a change of heart. We look at the relationships in our lives to see where we need God's help. Then we ask God for his grace to heal those relationships.

A New Heart

God tells us, "I will give them another heart and a new spirit…. I will remove the hearts of stone" (**Ezekiel 11:19**). Sin makes us less than who we were meant to be. If we are willing, God will help us to change. God didn't create us to have lives of sin without him. He created us to have amazing lives with him!

The Sacrament of Penance gives us God's forgiveness. It helps us change our hearts of stone into hearts for loving him and others.

The stone hearts show attitudes or actions that are not loving. Choose one non-loving action from each stone heart. Write a better, loving action for it in the purple heart.

1 Disobeying my parents

2 Being mean to a classmate

3 Not thanking God for who I am and what I have

4 Wanting to win so bad, I cheat

5 Being mad at my parents for not buying me everything I ask for

6 Not spending time with God by praying

Pray the closing prayer.

Reconciliation Space Find out what the Reconciliation room or confessional at your parish looks like. These spaces can be very different from church to church. It may be an open but private space for people to celebrate the Sacrament of Penance and Reconciliation. If it's an enclosed space, go inside. See where the priest sits and where a person who is confessing can sit or kneel.

When you get home, draw what this space looks like.

 Disciples Sharing Look for the Penitential Act in a hymnal or Missalette (if your parish has them). Or look to find it online at usccb.org in the *Roman Missal*. Discuss as a family what this prayer says about a change of heart and God's forgiveness.

Session videos, games, multimedia glossary, Sunday readings and backgrounds, Sacrament FAQs, reflections, and more at **sacraments.osv.com**

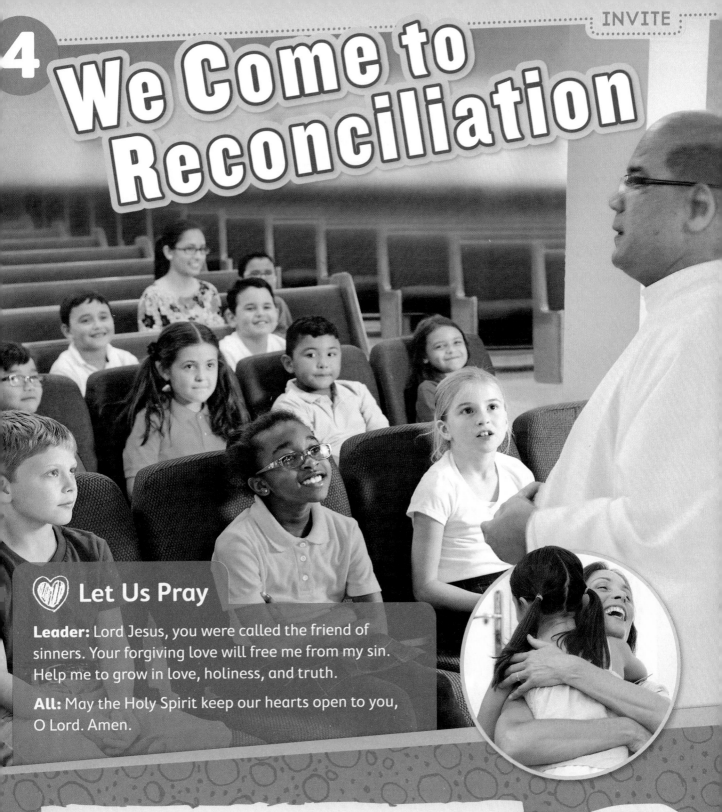

4 We Come to Reconciliation

💗 Let Us Pray

Leader: Lord Jesus, you were called the friend of sinners. Your forgiving love will free me from my sin. Help me to grow in love, holiness, and truth.

All: May the Holy Spirit keep our hearts open to you, O Lord. Amen.

God's Word

As the Father loves me, so I also love you. Remain in my love. If you keep my commandments, you will remain in my love, just as I have kept my Father's commandments and remain in his love.... This is my commandment: love one another as I love you.... You are my friends if you do what I command you. John 15:9–14

What did you hear God say to you today?

 Opening Video
sacraments.osv.com

Lost and Found

Work with a partner to find the hidden pictures. There are five in all: a dove, an action figure, rosary beads, a homework binder, and a teddy bear.

Have you ever lost something important because you didn't take good care of it? Maybe it was a special toy that you didn't put where it belonged. Or maybe you were too busy playing and didn't put your homework in your backpack.

What did you do when you realized it was lost? Did you ask for help to look for it? Did you find it? If so, what did you do when you found it?

Catholic Signs & Symbols

STOLES When you celebrate the Sacrament of Penance and Reconciliation, the priest is happy to see you. The priest is there to offer you God's forgiveness. He does this in the name of Jesus.

During this Sacrament, the priest wears a purple or violet stole. This special cloth looks something like a scarf. Purple and violet are signs of sorrow and the need to change our hearts.

Priests wear stoles while celebrating all of the Sacraments. The stole symbolizes the priest's office. It tells us that a priest or bishop is acting in the person of Christ.

Only bishops, priests, and deacons wear stoles.

Meet Jesus

THE GOOD SHEPHERD A shepherd takes care of sheep. He feeds them and keeps them safe.

Jesus once told his disciples the Parable of the Lost Sheep (see Luke 15:4–7). In this story, Jesus describes a shepherd who searches everywhere for one lost sheep. When he finds the sheep, the shepherd carries it home. He rejoices that it has been found. Jesus is our shepherd. If we get lost because we turn from God's love, he never gives up on us. Jesus will always search for us. He will bring us back to his Father!

The Shepherd and His Sheep

During Jesus' time, people knew a lot about being a shepherd. Many people were shepherds. When he called himself a shepherd, Jesus' listeners understood what he was trying to tell them.

God's Word

The Good Shepherd [Jesus said,] "... the sheep hear [the shepherd's] voice, as he calls his own sheep by name and leads them out.... He walks ahead of them, and the sheep follow him, because they recognize his voice. But they will not follow a stranger; they will run away from him, because they do not recognize the voice of strangers....

"I am the good shepherd. A good shepherd lays down his life for the sheep. A hired man, who is not a shepherd and whose sheep are not his own, sees a wolf coming and leaves the sheep and runs away, and the wolf catches and scatters them.... I am the good shepherd, and I know mine and mine know me, just as the Father knows me and I know the Father; and I will lay down my life for the sheep." John 10:3–5, 11–15

Jesus, Our Shepherd

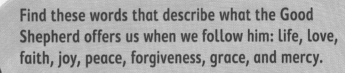

Jesus is the Good Shepherd. He was sent to us by his Father to guide us to him. The Holy Spirit helps us to recognize the voice of Jesus when he calls. Jesus will keep us safe. He will lead us to the Father's love.

Sometimes we *choose* to do what we know is wrong on purpose. We disobey God and we sin. This is different from a mistake or an accident, which are not sins. When we sin, we turn away from God and his love. This hurts our relationship with him and others. But Jesus never leaves us. He always calls us back to him.

Find these words that describe what the Good Shepherd offers us when we follow him: life, love, faith, joy, peace, forgiveness, grace, and mercy.

Entering the Mystery

Jesus told the parable of the shepherd and his sheep to teach us. He wants us to know that his Father never gives up on us. How blessed we are to have the Sacrament of Penance and Reconciliation. It allows us to experience God's forgiveness and mercy! With the help of the Holy Spirit, the Sacrament changes us. It brings us back to God and the Church. It reconciles us by making right our relationship with God and his Church.

The Rite of Penance

Penance and Reconciliation always has four main parts:

Confession
We confess our sins to the priest.

Contrition, or repentance
We are sorry for our sins. We promise to really try not to repeat those sins again.

Penance
We show through prayers and actions that we are truly sorry for our sins. We want to help repair the harm caused.

Absolution
The priest forgives us for our sins in God's name. Only priests can forgive sins in the name of Christ. Our sins are absolved, or forgiven. We are restored to a life of grace.

When we celebrate the Sacrament of Penance, we are called "penitents." Penitents are people who are sorry for their sins and ask for forgiveness. We come to be reconciled. We want to make right our relationships with God and others.

Most parishes have set times for people to come to the Sacrament. In this case, the Sacrament of Penance is celebrated by the priest and one penitent at a time.

Sometimes, parishes will have a large gathering of people to celebrate this Sacrament. This usually happens during Advent or Lent.

Either way, you always meet privately with a priest to confess your sins and receive absolution. This private meeting could take place in the open. Or it could take place in one of the corners of the sanctuary, rather than behind closed doors.

Contrition Before, During, and After

Contrition is necessary to receive this Sacrament. Contrition means being sorry for our sins and intending to try really hard not to sin again. Contrition starts before we get to the celebration of the Sacrament. We should feel "heartfelt sorrow." This means we are really sorry and sad about our sins.

The Holy Spirit works with our conscience, helping us know that what we did is wrong. We don't feel sorry because someone tells us to be sorry. It comes from the heart. This is what it means to be contrite.

To be reconciled with God, we must resolve not to sin again. We have to want to change. We have to say that we do not want to sin again. Because we love Christ, we want to become closer to him.

When you celebrate First Penance, it will be the first time that you hear the priest speak for Jesus and offer you the Father's forgiveness.

Celebrating Reconciliation Individually

Match each step of the Sacrament with its description.

Steps	Descriptions
Welcome & Sign of the Cross	The priest gives you a prayer or action to do after the Sacrament to show your sorrow and help repair the harm caused by sin.
Scripture	This is optional, but sometimes the priest will share a Bible story of forgiveness.
Confession	These are the words and gestures of the priest that grant forgiveness of our sins in Christ's name.
Penance	The priest welcomes you.
Contrition	You show you are sorry for your sins and will try not to sin again.
Absolution	You name or tell your sins to the priest.
Praise & Dismissal	The priest offers you God's peace and sends you forth.

The Act of Contrition

In the celebration of Reconciliation, we express our sorrow by saying the Act of Contrition. The Act of Contrition is the Prayer of Penitents. There are many versions of the Act of Contrition. Some are as simple as "Lord Jesus, Son of God, have mercy on me, a sinner." Below is a version that you can pray during the Sacrament. You can also say this prayer at home. It is good to pray the Act of Contrition after examining your conscience. ➡ *Go to pages 83–84 for other examples of prayers that show contrition.*

My God,
I am sorry for my sins
with all my heart.

In choosing to do wrong
and failing to do good,
I have sinned against you
whom I should love above
all things.

I firmly intend, with your help,
to do penance,
to sin no more,
and to avoid whatever
leads me to sin.

Our Savior Jesus Christ
suffered and died for us.

In his name, my God,
have mercy. Amen.

Disciples Sharing *Talk about what each part of the Act of Contrition means.*

Changing How We Live

The grace we receive in the Sacrament of Penance helps our hearts to be changed. We grow closer to God. We honor God's laws when we are loving to our neighbors, friends, and family. True contrition changes how we treat each other.

Fill in the title and boxes below. Make an illustrated story about contrition. You can use your own experience or make up a story.

Title: _____

One day, I hurt someone by _____
_____ .

…at the person said …en I hurt him or her:

What I felt when I realized I had hurt the person:

This is how it ended:

 Pray the closing prayer.

My Family in Our Parish

We Come to Reconciliation

Participating in Reconciliation Your parish likely has scheduled times for individual Reconciliation. Check your parish bulletin for these times. Many parishes have times set aside on Saturday. This is usually in the afternoon, before the Vigil Mass. As a family, plan to visit the parish. While the adults celebrate Reconciliation, the children can pray for them. They can also pray for other penitents who are waiting to celebrate the Sacrament.

Together, in the space below, write two short prayers for your child to pray while you are at church.

Disciples Sharing Discuss the importance of prayer. When are some times that your family prays together? When are some times that you pray alone?

Session videos, games, multimedia glossary, Sunday readings and backgrounds, Sacrament FAQs, reflections, and more at **sacraments.osv.com**

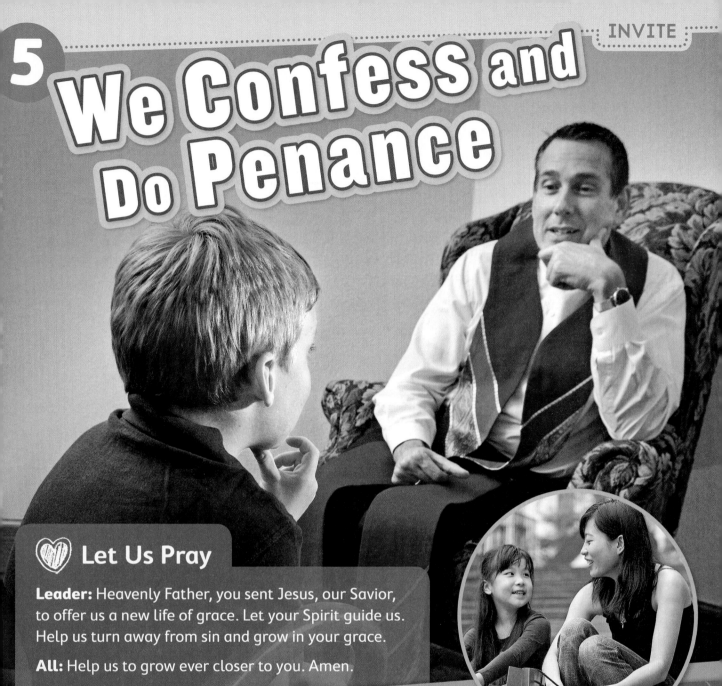

5 We Confess and Do Penance

♡ Let Us Pray

Leader: Heavenly Father, you sent Jesus, our Savior, to offer us a new life of grace. Let your Spirit guide us. Help us turn away from sin and grow in your grace.

All: Help us to grow ever closer to you. Amen.

God's Word

Jesus [said], "Whoever loves me will keep my word, and my Father will love him, and we will come to him and make our dwelling with him. Whoever does not love me does not keep my words.... I have told you this while I am with you. The Advocate, the holy Spirit that the Father will send in my name—he will teach you everything and remind you of all that [I] told you." John 14:23–26

What did you hear God say to you today?

Opening Video
sacraments.osv.com

Using Our Hands

Has there ever been a time when you couldn't use your hands? Maybe you had to wear a cast. Maybe you had your hand wrapped because you were injured. We do many things with our hands. When we can't use them, there are a lot of things that can be hard to do!

Inside the outline below, describe an activity you would like to do with your hands.

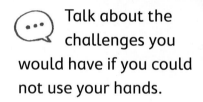

Talk about the challenges you would have if you could not use your hands.

Catholic Signs & Symbols

HANDS Using your hands is an important part of the Sacrament of Penance and Reconciliation. By opening the door to meet the priest, you show that your heart is ready for God's grace. You use your hands to make the Sign of the Cross. You fold your hands in prayer to show honor and respect to God.

Jesus used his hands in many ways, too. He used his hands to heal those who were sick and to forgive sins. At the end of the Sacrament of Penance, the priest holds his hands over your head or towards you. Then he says the Prayer of Absolution. This is the Church's prayer of forgiveness. It offers you Jesus' mercy and love.

Hand extended in absolution

Meet Jesus

CHRIST THE KING We call Jesus "Christ the King." A good king knows what his people need. He makes laws so his people are kept safe and are cared for. A good king serves his people.

Jesus was never the king of a country. He is the King of our hearts and lives. He invites all people to turn away from sin and enter into the **Kingdom of God**. This Kingdom is the world of love, peace, and justice that is in heaven and is still being built on Earth. When we celebrate the Sacraments, we are in the presence of our King!

51

INVITED INTO THE KINGDOM

During Jesus' time on Earth, kings were anointed. They had special oil poured on their heads. This was a sign that they were chosen to be the leader. When we say Jesus Christ, we are calling Jesus "the anointed one."

Jesus was chosen by God the Father to establish a new Kingdom. He was "anointed" by the Holy Spirit. Jesus wants everyone to join him in God's Kingdom.

Oil for anointing

God's Word

Zacchaeus the Tax Collector Now a man there named Zacchaeus, who was a chief tax collector and also a wealthy man, was seeking to see who Jesus was; but he could not see him because of the crowd, for he was short.... So he ran ahead and climbed a sycamore tree in order to see Jesus, who was about to pass that way. When he reached the place, Jesus looked up and said to him, "Zacchaeus, come down quickly, for today I must stay at your house." And he came down quickly and received him with joy. When they all saw this, they began to grumble, saying, "He has gone to stay at the house of a sinner." But Zacchaeus stood there and said to the Lord, "Behold, half of my possessions, Lord, I shall give to the poor, and if I have extorted anything from anyone I shall repay it four times over." And Jesus said to him, "Today salvation has come to this house.... For the Son of Man has come to seek and to save what was lost." Luke 19:2–10

The Spirit Leads Us

Help Zacchaeus find the tree so he can hear Jesus' Good News. Then lead Zacchaeus to the people at the end of the maze so that he can repay them.

Zacchaeus wants to see Jesus so much that he climbs a tree! When Jesus says he wants to visit with him, Zacchaeus's heart is filled with joy. He has a change of heart. We call this a **conversion**. Conversion is responding to God's love and forgiveness. It is turning away from sin. Zacchaeus admits that his life must change. He offers to help repair the harm he caused.

When we listen for the voice of the Holy Spirit, we find true joy, just as Zacchaeus did.

Entering the Mystery

Jesus invited Zacchaeus to a new life. This new life is filled with love and friendship. God doesn't wait until we change before he loves us. God loves us just as we are. God's love and grace move us to conversion. We change. We become more like Jesus.

It is wonderful to know God's love. This love brings you to the Sacrament of Penance. God forgives you. His love will help you become the person he made you to be.

The Heart of Reconciliation

When we sin, we harm our relationship with Jesus and others. When we are truly sorry for our sins, we have contrition. Through our contrition, the Holy Spirit calls us to the Sacrament of Penance. In this Sacrament, we can be reconciled with God and one another.

After contrition, the next two parts of the Sacrament are confession and penance. These steps lead us to further change our hearts.

Confession

When we do what is wrong on purpose, we sin. We say "no" to God. Some sins are more serious than others because they do more harm. A **mortal sin** is a serious sin. It causes a person's relationship with God to be broken. In a mortal sin, we completely turn our backs on God and his love.

A **venial sin** hurts a person's friendship with God but does not completely break it. Venial sins pull us away from God. They also harm our relationships with others.

To confess means to admit something. In the Sacrament of Penance, **confession** is when we tell our sins to the priest. This can make us feel uncomfortable. Yet, we trust that God loves us no matter what.

God, through the priest, lovingly hears us. The priest helps us experience God's merciful love. It is not easy to admit our sins. But the sins we tell the priest stay with him. He cannot share our confession with anyone.

Penance

We need to *say* we are sorry for our sins. We must also *show* that we are truly sorry. In this Sacrament, this is done through **penance**. Penance is a prayer or action to help us repair the harm caused by our sins. It helps us make things right.

The priest gives us penance. Penance is usually something we pray, do, or give up after the celebration of the Sacrament. It helps us get into better habits for following Jesus.

The **Works of Mercy** are sometimes given as a penance. This could be feeding the hungry, visiting the sick, comforting the sad, and forgiving others. The Works of Mercy show care for the physical and spiritual needs of others. Jesus calls us to follow his example. We should act with mercy all the time, not just as a penance.

➡ Go to page 78 for a list of the Corporal and Spiritual Works of Mercy.

By "doing penance," we grow more like Christ. Our hearts are opened to God's grace and mercy. We use our hands and hearts to help repair harm.

> **The Church wants us to experience God's saving love.**
>
> We are strongly encouraged to confess venial sins. We *must* confess mortal sins and receive absolution in order to be reconciled with God and with the Church.

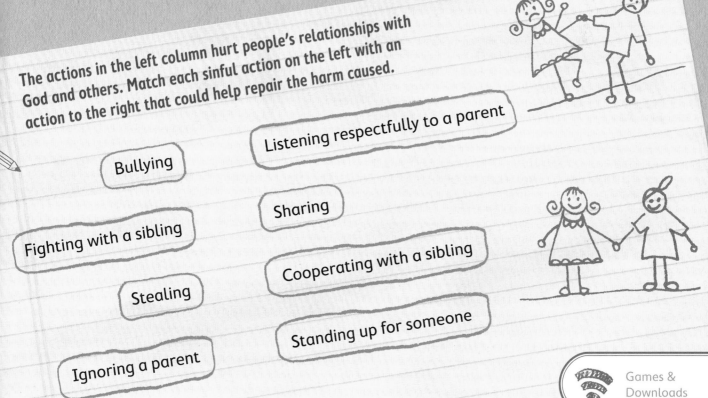

The actions in the left column hurt people's relationships with God and others. Match each sinful action on the left with an action to the right that could help repair the harm caused.

Bullying

Listening respectfully to a parent

Fighting with a sibling

Sharing

Cooperating with a sibling

Stealing

Standing up for someone

Ignoring a parent

Games & Downloads

RECONCILIATION IS A JOURNEY

Who is with you as you grow and learn? Who helps you when you've hurt others? Who shows you love? Where do you become closer to Jesus? In the spaces below, write the names of people who help you along the way.

Sometimes we gather as a group or parish to celebrate Reconciliation. This liturgy includes scripture readings. It also includes time for an examination of conscience and for group prayer. Then there is individual confession and absolution. Whether it is communal or individual, when we come to the Sacrament, the whole Church rejoices. ➡ *Go to page 70 to learn more about celebrating the Sacrament with several penitents.*

The Sacrament of Reconciliation is part of our journey back to God. Others are with us on this journey. The things we say and do affect them, too.

Together, we are on our way to live forever with God in heaven. Our happiness each day comes from living as Jesus' disciples. We cannot even begin to imagine the happiness of living with God forever!

In God's Kingdom

A good king loves and protects his people. We know that Jesus loves and protects us. He serves us, too. Jesus gives us Commandments to follow. His Commandments help us know how to live as his brothers and sisters. He calls us to live according to his New Commandment— to love others the way he has loved us.

Inside the boundaries of the kingdom below, describe the attitudes or actions of someone who follows the laws of God's Kingdom. Outside the boundaries, write some attitudes or actions that are not part of the Kingdom of God.

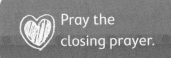 Pray the closing prayer.

My Family *in* Our Parish

We Confess and Do Penance

Models of Faith Is your parish named after a saint? If not, are there any pictures or statues of saints in your church? Saints were ordinary people, just like you and me. But they did extraordinary things with God's help. They followed God's laws and shared his Kingdom with others. They did this through their words and actions.

Find out who your Church's patron saint is or choose another saint. Draw or paste a picture of that saint in the space below.

Find some information about your saint.
Write one fact about him or her.

 Disciples Sharing What did you learn from this saint about living a life of conversion and reconciliation?

Session videos, games, multimedia glossary, Sunday readings and backgrounds, Sacrament FAQs, reflections, and more at **sacraments.osv.com**

6

We Are Forgiven and We Forgive

Let Us Pray

Leader: Almighty God, you are merciful and kind. Through the power of your Spirit, help us to share your love and forgiveness with those around us.

All: Happy are those whose sins are forgiven and who live in peace. Amen.

God's Word

The disciples rejoiced when they saw the Lord. [Jesus] said to them again, "Peace be with you. As the Father has sent me, so I send you." And when he had said this, he breathed on them and said to them, "Receive the holy Spirit. Whose sins you forgive are forgiven them, and whose sins you retain are retained."

John 20:20b–23

What did you hear God say to you today?

Opening Video
sacraments.osv.com

59

Signs of Community

God created us to be in relationship with others. Communities are one of the ways we live in relationship. We belong to some communities for a short time. We belong to other communities forever, like our family. You belong to God's family forever because you were baptized into his Church.

The Holy Spirit connects us to Christ and one another. In the Church, we experience the love of the Holy Trinity. We belong to this community of faith. The Church guides us and cares for us. In this community, we share God's love with others.

Disciples Sharing *Look at the pictures. Talk about ways the Church is a community. What are some ways the Church is a sign of God's love?*

Catholic Signs & Symbols

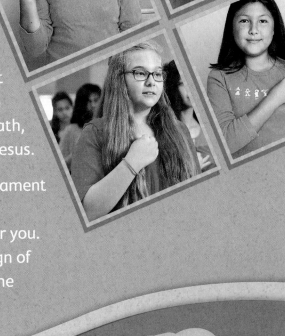

SIGN OF THE CROSS

We make the Sign of the Cross when we begin and end our prayers. We make the Sign of the Cross on ourselves. Priests bless us by making the Sign of the Cross on us or over us. Our parents mark us with the Sign of the Cross. They do this at our Baptism and throughout our lives.

When we make the Sign of the Cross, we are remembering the three Divine Persons of the Holy Trinity. We recall that we are saved through the life, suffering, Death, and Resurrection of Jesus.

At the end of the Sacrament of Penance, the priest extends his hands over you. Then he makes the Sign of the Cross as he says the words of absolution.

Meet Jesus

JESUS AND HIS BODY, THE CHURCH Through the power of the Holy Spirit, Jesus formed his disciples into his own Body. This happened after his Death and Resurrection. Saint Paul tells us that Jesus is the head of the Body.

As members of his Church, we know that our life comes from Jesus. We live in him. When we are baptized, we become one with him. We become members of the **Body of Christ**. We are joined to Jesus and all the people who have faith in him. Jesus lives *in* his Church. We live *for* him.

Sacraments and the Body of Christ

Jesus is always with us. We are his Body on Earth. He is with us in a special way in every Sacrament. In the Sacraments, Jesus offers us his life. He gives us his grace. This helps us grow deeper in our love for God and for one another. The Sacraments help us to grow in faith, love, and holiness. They help us grow stronger as the Body of Christ.

In the Sacraments, Jesus continues to teach and speak his Word to us. Jesus tells us how we are to live.

God's Word

How Often Must We Forgive? [Jesus said,] "For where two or three are gathered together in my name, there am I in the midst of them." Then Peter approaching asked him, "Lord, if my brother sins against me, how often must I forgive him? As many as seven times?" Jesus answered, "I say to you, not seven times but seventy-seven times." Matthew 18:20–22

BE FORGIVEN AND FORGIVE

Imagine that you are Peter. You've just asked Jesus a question. You think that forgiving someone seven times seems like a lot. Jesus' answer probably catches you by surprise.

Seventy-seven is a pretty big number. Jesus uses this big number to show that we must always offer forgiveness. This is because Jesus always forgave others no matter what.

Forgiveness is a choice. It is an act of love. When we forgive, we decide not to allow a person's actions or words to get in the way of our love. We choose to let love be stronger.

Choosing to offer forgiveness can sometimes be hard. Put a check mark next to one of the situations described below. Then tell or act out what you would do to offer forgiveness.

- ☐ Someone borrows my book or toy and loses it.
- ☐ Someone makes fun of me.
- ☐ I make a mistake and my friend laughs at me.
- ☐ A person I know tells a lie about me.
- ☐ Someone breaks a promise to me.
- ☐ Someone takes something from me without asking.

Entering the Mystery

Saint Paul tells us that love "does not brood over injury" (**1 Corinthians 13:5**). He is telling us that God does not hold on to the things we have done wrong. He lets them go. He forgives us. In the Sacrament of Penance, we are given the grace to do the same thing. This grace helps us to live in God's peace and joy.

God Forgives Us

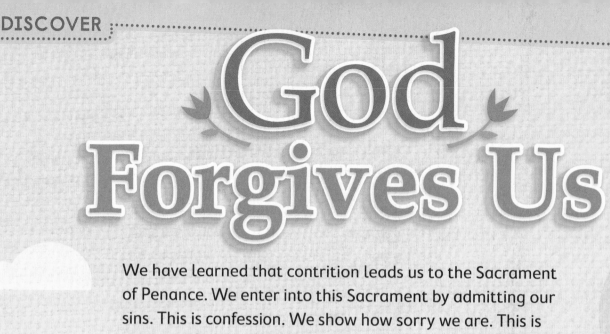

We have learned that contrition leads us to the Sacrament of Penance. We enter into this Sacrament by admitting our sins. This is confession. We show how sorry we are. This is penance. Our hearts are opened and we are prepared to receive God's mercy. These are the steps that lead us, the penitents, to absolution or forgiveness.

The final part rests in the hands of God. This is done through the Church and her minister, the priest. After you confess your sins, the priest extends his hands (or just his right hand) over your head. Then he says a **Prayer of Absolution**. The priest grants forgiveness of our sins in God's name.

God, the Father of mercies

Through the death and resurrection of his Son has reconciled the world to himself

And sent the Holy Spirit among us for the forgiveness of sins

The Sacrament is not just a sign of God's forgiveness. It's the source of it. It brings about forgiveness because of God's never-ending love. Sin causes damage to our relationships with God and others. If one part of the Body is suffering, we all suffer in some way.

We come to this Sacrament because we are sorry. We want our hearts to be changed. We confess our sins to the priest who is the minister of Christ and his Church. We promise to sin no more. We receive our penance. Then, by the priest's words and actions, our sins are forgiven. And we are forgiven for the hurt we have caused others. God gives us something we can see and hear so that we know in our minds and hearts that he is forgiving us.

This is a moment of joy. We are restored to right relationship with both God and the community. The priest may say, "Give thanks to the Lord, for he is good." With joy, we reply, "His mercy endures for ever." The priest then dismisses us, usually telling us to "Go in peace" (*Rite of Penance*, 47).

Disciples Sharing *How do you feel when someone forgives you? How do you feel when you forgive someone else? How does knowing that God always loves you, even when you have sinned, make you feel?*

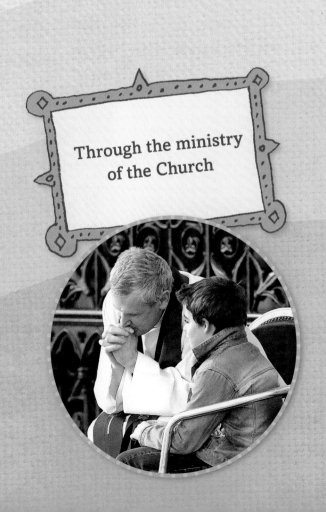

Through the ministry of the Church

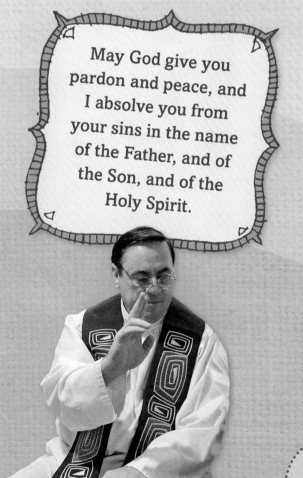

May God give you pardon and peace, and I absolve you from your sins in the name of the Father, and of the Son, and of the Holy Spirit.

Steps for Celebrating Reconciliation

It's exciting to prepare to celebrate the Sacrament of Penance for the first time. This Sacrament is a joyful gift from God and the Church. We need this Sacrament. It helps prepare us to celebrate other Sacraments. It helps us to live as members of the Body of Christ.

How will your parish celebrate your First Penance? You may be with other children as you prepare to celebrate as a group. The Sacrament may also be celebrated individually. ➡ *To review the celebration of the Sacrament with several penitents, go to page 70. For the individual celebration, go to page 73.*

Steps in the Sacrament

Number the steps in the correct order.

◯ Examine my conscience

◯ Receive my penance

◯ Say the Act of Contrition

◯ Respond to the priest's welcome

◯ Do my penance

◯ Be absolved by the priest

◯ Read Scripture

◯ Confess my sins

◯ Give praise to God

◯ Rejoice

Games & Downloads

Sent in Christ's Peace

When we celebrate the Sacrament of Penance, the whole Church rejoices. We have had a change of heart. God has given us peace! He asks us to be peacemakers in the world. We can do this by choosing to forgive others. We can act with love toward those who have harmed us.

People also experience peace when they have what they need. As the Body of Christ, we pray and work so that all families have what they need. We pray and work to stop people from harming each other. We pray and work so that everyone can hear Jesus' invitation to live in his Kingdom.

Imagine that Jesus is sending you out to give the gift of peace to others. There are many ways to do this. The Works of Mercy show us some. Pick two works from page 78. Write them on the labels for each gift. Then fill in the *To* and *From* tags.

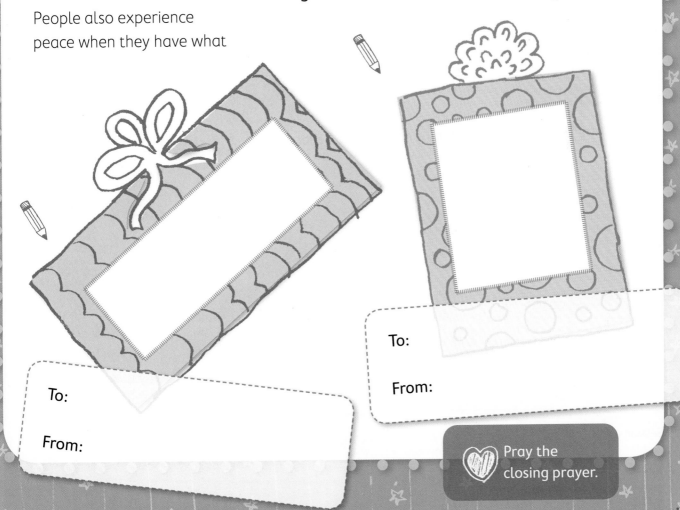

To:

From:

To:

From:

Pray the closing prayer.

My Family *in* Our Parish

We Are Forgiven and We Forgive

Being Peacemakers At the end of Mass, be sure to take a parish bulletin. At home, search the bulletin with your parents. Look for the people and groups in your parish who are peacemakers. They are the ones who are making meals, making clothes, and holding prayer vigils. They are educating others about important topics. They are finding ways to help your community.

List some of these people or groups here:

What does your family do to bring peace to others?

 Disciples Sharing How can you do more? Choose one group in your parish that you can join. Or think of another way that you and your family can be peacemakers.

Session videos, games, multimedia glossary, Sunday readings and backgrounds, Sacrament FAQs, reflections, and more at **sacraments.osv.com**

The Seven Sacraments

The Catholic Church celebrates Seven Sacraments—special signs and celebrations of Jesus' presence. Jesus gave us the Sacraments to allow us to share in God's life and work.

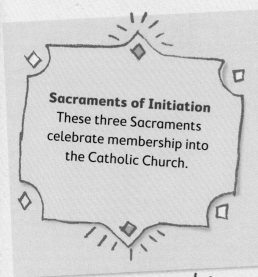

Sacraments of Initiation
These three Sacraments celebrate membership into the Catholic Church.

• **Baptism:** By the power of the Holy Spirit, we receive new life in Christ, our sins are forgiven, and we become part of Christ's Body here on Earth, the Church.

• **Confirmation:** We are sealed with the Gifts of the Holy Spirit, who deepens the life of Christ given to us in Baptism and strengthens us to be witnesses of Christ's saving love.

• **Eucharist:** Jesus shares his life with us in the bread and wine that become his Body and Blood. We grow closer to Jesus and one another. We receive the grace to become more like Christ and to live as his disciples.

Sacraments of Healing
In these Sacraments, God's forgiveness and healing are given to those suffering physical and spiritual sickness.

• **Penance and Reconciliation:** Through our sorrowful hearts and our desire to change, as well as the actions of the priest, God forgives our sins, and our relationships with God and others are healed.

• **Anointing of the Sick:** Through prayer and anointing with holy oil by the priest, God gives strength, grace, comfort, and peace to the sick. And for those who are not also able to receive Penance, their sins are forgiven.

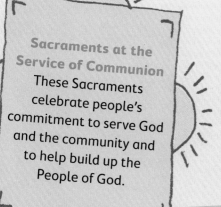

Sacraments at the Service of Communion
These Sacraments celebrate people's commitment to serve God and the community and to help build up the People of God.

• **Holy Orders:** God calls men to be bishops, priests, and deacons who are ordained to teach, lead, and serve the Church. Ordained men are anointed with Sacred Chrism and are marked forever as Christ's representatives.

• **Matrimony (Marriage):** A baptized man and a baptized woman make a promise to help each other grow in holiness and to love each other as Jesus loves his Church. They promise to be faithful to each other.

Penance and Reconciliation
Group Celebration

We are given the opportunity to experience God's love, mercy, and forgiveness in the Sacrament of Penance and Reconciliation. If you are truly sorry, God will forgive any sins you have committed.

Here are the four steps of this Sacrament when it's celebrated with other people. We do everything together except individual confession and absolution.

1. Introductory Rites

Usually we begin with a song. Then the priest says some words of greeting or welcome and an opening prayer.

2. Celebration of the Word of God

Scripture is proclaimed, as it is during Mass. We hear readings about showing sorrow, forgiveness, and God's mercy. There may also be a short homily. We may be invited to spend some time examining our conscience.

3. Rite of Reconciliation

After we have had time for reflection or to examine our conscience, we are invited to pray together as a community.

LECTIONARY

Together, we express our sorrow and desire to be forgiven by saying the Act of Contrition. (Sometimes the Act of Contrition is prayed individually inside the confessional or Reconciliation room.)

Act of Contrition (Traditional)

My God,
I am sorry for my sins with all my heart.
In choosing to do wrong
and failing to do good,
I have sinned against you
whom I should love above all things.
I firmly intend, with your help,
to do penance,
to sin no more,
and to avoid whatever leads me to sin.
Our Savior Jesus Christ
suffered and died for us.
In his name, my God, have mercy.

Oración del penitente (Tradicional)

Dios mío, me arrepiento de todo corazón
de todo lo malo que he hecho
y de todo lo bueno que he dejado de hacer,
porque pecando te he ofendido a ti,
que eres el sumo bien
y digno de ser amado sobre todas las cosas.
Propongo firmemente, con tu gracia,
cumplir la penitencia,
no volver a pecar
y evitar las ocasiones de pecado.
Perdóname, Señor, por los méritos
de la pasión de nuestro Salvador Jesucristo.

Then we pray the Lord's Prayer together as a group (see page 82).

Next, each penitent meets individually with a priest for confession. This is when you tell the priest your sins. Remember, he can never tell anyone else. Then the priest talks with you about penance, or something you can do to help repair some of the harm caused by your sin. He talks with you about how to change so that you love God and others more.

The priest, who acts in Christ's name, will then extend his hands and pray the Prayer of Absolution. This prayer offers you God's forgiveness. Here are the words of the prayer.

Prayer of Absolution

God, the Father of mercies,
through the death and resurrection of his Son
has reconciled the world to himself
and sent the Holy Spirit among us
for the forgiveness of sins;
through the ministry of the Church
may God give you pardon and peace,
and I absolve you from your sins
in the name of the Father, and of the Son,
and of the Holy Spirit.

Oración de absolución

Dios, Padre misericordioso,
que reconcilió al mundo consigo
por la muerte y la resurrección de su Hijo
y envió al Espíritu Santo para el perdón de los pecados,
te conceda, por el ministerio de la Iglesia,
el perdón y la paz.
Y yo te absuelvo de tus pecados,
en el nombre del Padre, y del Hijo,
y del Espíritu Santo.

Once everyone has had a chance to meet individually with a priest, the priest leading the celebration encourages us to give thanks for God's mercy and do good works.

4. Concluding Rites

This part of the Sacrament could include a blessing and dismissal. We are sent to go forth, living in God's peace.

Penance and Reconciliation
Individual Celebration

The Sacrament of Penance and Reconciliation can be celebrated individually. Below are the steps for the individual celebration of this Rite.

Examination of Conscience

Before we seek God's forgiveness in the Sacrament, we prepare with an examination of conscience. We ask the Holy Spirit to help us think about our actions. We can ask ourselves, "How well have I followed the Ten Commandments, the Great Commandment, and the Beatitudes?" This helps us to see where we really need a change of heart.

1. Welcome

The priest greets you and makes the Sign of the Cross.

2. Reading of the Word of God

Sometimes the priest reads a scripture story about forgiveness.

3. Confession and Penance

You tell the priest your sins. Remember, he can never tell anyone else. Then the priest talks with you about penance, or something you can do to help repair some of the harm caused by your sins. He talks with you about how to change so that you love God and others more.

4. Contrition and Absolution

You pray an Act of Contrition. You say this prayer to show you are sorry for your sins and will try not to sin again.

Act of Contrition (Traditional)
My God,
I am sorry for my sins with all my heart.
In choosing to do wrong
and failing to do good,
I have sinned against you
whom I should love above all things.
I firmly intend, with your help,
to do penance,
to sin no more,
and to avoid whatever leads me to sin.
Our Savior Jesus Christ
suffered and died for us.
In his name, my God, have mercy.

Oración del penitente (Tradicional)
Dios mío, me arrepiento de todo corazón
de todo lo malo que he hecho
y de todo lo bueno que he dejado de hacer,
porque pecando te he ofendido a ti,
que eres el sumo bien
y digno de ser amado sobre todas las cosas.
Propongo firmemente, con tu gracia,
cumplir la penitencia,
no volver a pecar
y evitar las ocasiones de pecado.
Perdóname, Señor, por los méritos
de la pasión de nuestro Salvador Jesucristo.

PENANCE

The priest, who acts in Christ's name, will then extend his hands and pray the Prayer of Absolution. This prayer offers you God's forgiveness. Below are the words of the prayer.

Prayer of Absolution

God, the Father of mercies,
through the death and resurrection of his Son
has reconciled the world to himself
and sent the Holy Spirit among us
for the forgiveness of sins;
through the ministry of the Church
may God give you pardon and peace,
and I absolve you from your sins
in the name of the Father, and of the Son,
and of the Holy Spirit.

Oración de absolución

Dios, Padre misericordioso,
que reconcilió al mundo consigo
por la muerte y la resurrección de su Hijo
y envió al Espíritu Santo para el perdón de los pecados,
te conceda, por el ministerio de la Iglesia,
el perdón y la paz.
Y yo te absuelvo de tus pecados,
en el nombre del Padre, y del Hijo,
y del Espíritu Santo.

5. Proclamation of Praise and Dismissal

The priest offers you God's peace and encourages you to do better in the future. He may end by saying, "Give thanks to the Lord, for he is good." You respond, "His mercy endures for ever" (*Rite of Penance*, 47). Then the priest sends you out to go in peace and share God's love with others.

Morality

The Ten Commandments

These are the laws God gave to Moses on Mount Sinai to show us how to live and what is necessary in order to love God and others.

	The Ten Commandments	Their Meaning
1	I am the Lord your God: you shall not have strange gods before me.	Keep God first in your life.
2	You shall not take the name of the Lord your God in vain.	Always use God's name in a reverent way.
3	Remember to keep holy the Lord's Day.	Attend Mass and rest on Sunday.
4	Honor your father and your mother.	Obey your parents and guardians.
5	You shall not kill.	Be kind to the people and animals God made; care for yourself and others.
6	You shall not commit adultery.	Be respectful in the things you do with your body.
7	You shall not steal.	Take care of other people's things; don't take what belongs to someone else. Respect other people and their property.
8	You shall not bear false witness against your neighbor.	Respect others by always telling the truth.
9	You shall not covet your neighbor's wife.	Keep your thoughts and words clean; don't be jealous of other people's friendships.
10	You shall not covet your neighbor's goods.	Be happy with the things you have; don't be jealous of what other people have.

The Great Commandment

This twofold Commandment sums up all of God's laws:

"You shall love the Lord, your God, with all your heart, with all your being, with all your strength, and with all your mind, and your neighbor as yourself." Luke 10:27

The Beatitudes

The Beatitudes are Jesus' main teachings about the love and care that you are called to show to God and others. They show us the way to true happiness in God's Kingdom.

Blessed are the poor in spirit,
  for theirs is the kingdom of heaven.
Blessed are they who mourn,
  for they will be comforted.
Blessed are the meek,
  for they will inherit the land.
Blessed are they who hunger and thirst
  for righteousness,
  for they will be satisfied.
Blessed are the merciful,
  for they will be shown mercy.
Blessed are the clean of heart,
  for they will see God.
Blessed are the peacemakers,
  for they will be called children of God.
Blessed are they who are persecuted
  for the sake of righteousness,
  for theirs is the kingdom of heaven.
Matthew 5:3–10

Jesus' New Commandment

Jesus loved his disciples by serving them and giving of himself to them. He gave them this New Commandment:

"Love one another. As I have loved you, so you also should love one another."
John 13:34

Morality

Precepts of the Church

The following precepts are some of the responsibilities of members of the Catholic Church. The Church's leaders created these to help you understand the least you should do to deepen your relationship with God and the Church. As Catholics, we have a duty to live according to these teachings.

1 **Take part in Mass on Sundays and holy days. Keep these days holy and avoid unnecessary work.**
This precept makes sure that you take time to be with Jesus and your parish community, strengthens your faith, rests your body, and encourages you to enjoy God's creation.

2 **Celebrate the Sacrament of Penance and Reconciliation at least once a year.**
This precept helps you see how you need God's forgiveness and how you may need to grow in the way you think or act.

3 **Receive Holy Communion at least once a year during the Easter season.**
This precept strengthens your faith and makes you one with Jesus.

4 **Fast and abstain on days of penance.**
This precept helps you share in the sacrifice of Jesus, train yourself spiritually, and experience the hunger of the poor.

5 **Give your time, gifts, and money to support the Church.**
This precept encourages you to support the Church and participate in her works.

Corporal and Spiritual Works of Mercy

The Corporal Works of Mercy help us take care of the physical needs of others. The Spiritual Works of Mercy guide us to care for the spiritual needs of others.

Corporal
- Feed the hungry
- Give drink to the thirsty
- Clothe the naked
- Shelter the homeless
- Visit the sick
- Visit the imprisoned

Spiritual
- Warn the sinner
- Teach the ignorant
- Counsel the doubtful
- Comfort the sorrowful
- Bear wrongs patiently
- Forgive injuries
- Pray for the living and the dead

Virtues

Virtues are good spiritual habits or qualities that make you stronger and help you do what is right and good. Practicing virtue can give you the strength to make loving choices.

Theological Virtues

FAITH	This virtue makes it possible to believe in God and all that he has shown and taught us. It helps us to obey him.
HOPE	This virtue helps us trust in what God has shown and taught us. It helps us look forward to the happiness of life forever with God in heaven and the coming of his Kingdom on Earth.
CHARITY (Love)	This virtue helps us show our love for God by praising him, making him our top priority, showing love to our neighbors, and treating all of God's creation with kindness and respect.

Cardinal Virtues

PRUDENCE	This virtue helps us to be practical and make correct decisions about what is right and good with the help of the Holy Spirit and a well-formed conscience.
JUSTICE	This virtue helps us give God and others what is due to them.
FORTITUDE	This virtue helps us show courage and have strength during difficult times.
TEMPERANCE	This virtue helps us to use moderation, be disciplined, and have self-control.

Place sticker here

Place sticker here

Place sticker here

Place sticker here

Place sticker here

Examination of Conscience

In order to prepare for the Sacrament of Penance and Reconciliation, we begin by examining our conscience. Our conscience is God's gift to us that helps us know and choose right from wrong. For help with examining your conscience, follow these steps:

★ Begin by praying to the Holy Spirit to help you examine your conscience.

★ Think about the laws, rules, and guidance God has given us to help us know right from wrong and to love as he loves:

- the Ten Commandments
- the Beatitudes
- the Great Commandment
- the New Commandment
- the Precepts of the Church

★ Ask yourself questions like the ones on this page and the next. They will help you know whether what you've done, or have not done, is good or bad, right or wrong.

For Younger Children

Love of God

- Have I spent time with God by praying and paying attention and participating during Mass?
- Have I spoken God's name respectfully?
- Have I thanked God for the many gifts he has given me?

Love of Family, Neighbor, and Neighborhood

- Have I respected and obeyed my parents and all those who love and care for me?
- Have I been loving to my family and friends and all those around me?
- Have I been helpful to others, especially those in need?
- Have I respected the Earth and the environment?

Love of Self

- Have I taken good care of myself (eating properly, getting enough sleep)?
- Have I used my time wisely?
- Have I thought about the ways I can use the gifts and talents God has given me so that I can be a gift to others?

For Older Children

Love of God

- Have I made God a priority in my life? Are there things more important to me than God?
- Have I spent time in prayer?
- Do I pay attention and actively participate in Mass?
- Do I spend time reading and studying God's Word?
- Have I thanked God for the blessings in my life?
- Do I start each day by remembering the awesomeness of God and acknowledging that he has a purpose for my life?

Love of Family, Neighbor, and Neighborhood

- Have I respected and obeyed my parents, teachers, and all those who love and care for me?
- Have I been forgiving?
- Have I been fair to others? Do I hold grudges?
- Do I look for opportunities each day to be helpful to everyone around me?
- Do I speak well of others?

Love of Self

- Do I treat my body with respect, as a wondrous gift from God?
- Do I get enough exercise, eat properly, avoid things that are bad for me, and take care of my body?
- Am I careful that what I read, watch, and listen to help me to become the person God made me to be?

Prayers

Sign of the Cross
In the name of the Father,
and of the Son,
and of the Holy Spirit.
Amen.

Señal de la Cruz
En el nombre del Padre,
y del Hijo,
y del Espíritu Santo.
Amén.

The Lord's Prayer
Our Father, who art in heaven,
hallowed be thy name;
thy kingdom come,
thy will be done
on earth as it is in heaven.
Give us this day our daily bread,
and forgive us our trespasses,
as we forgive those who trespass against us;
and lead us not into temptation,
but deliver us from evil.
Amen.

El Padre Nuestro
Padre nuestro, que estás en el cielo,
santificado sea tu Nombre;
venga a nosotros tu reino;
hágase tu voluntad
   en la tierra como en el cielo.
Danos hoy nuestro pan de cada día;
perdona nuestras ofensas,
como también nosotros perdonamos
a los que nos ofenden;
no nos dejes caer en la tentación,
y líbranos del mal.
Amén.

The Hail Mary
Hail, Mary, full of grace,
the Lord is with thee.
Blessed art thou among women
and blessed is the fruit of thy womb, Jesus.
Holy Mary, Mother of God,
pray for us sinners,
now and at the hour of our death.
Amen.

Ave María
Dios te salve, María, llena eres de gracia;
 el Señor es contigo.
   Bendita Tú eres entre todas las mujeres,
      y bendito es el fruto de tu vientre, Jesús.
      Santa María, Madre de Dios,
         ruega por nosotros, pecadores,
         ahora y en la hora de nuestra muerte.
            Amén.

Act of Contrition (Traditional)

My God,
I am sorry for my sins with all my heart.
In choosing to do wrong
and failing to do good,
I have sinned against you
whom I should love above all things.
I firmly intend, with your help,
to do penance,
to sin no more,
and to avoid whatever leads me to sin.
Our Savior Jesus Christ
suffered and died for us.
In his name, my God, have mercy.

Oración del penitente (Tradicional)

Dios mío, me arrepiento de todo corazón
de todo lo malo que he hecho
y de todo lo bueno que he dejado de hacer,
porque pecando te he ofendido a ti,
que eres el sumo bien
y digno de ser amado sobre todas las cosas.
Propongo firmemente, con tu gracia,
cumplir la penitencia,
no volver a pecar
y evitar las ocasiones de pecado.
Perdóname, Señor, por los méritos
de la pasión de nuestro Salvador Jesucristo.

Act of Contrition (Alternate)

O my God,
I am sorry for my sins.
In choosing to sin, and failing to do good,
I have sinned against you and your Church.
I firmly intend
with the help of your Son
to make up for my sins
and to love, as I should.
Amen.

Oración del penitente (Alternativa)

¡Oh Dios mío, me arrepiento de corazón de
haberte ofendido, y detesto mis pecados, porque
temo la pérdida del cielo y los tormentos
del infierno, pero especialmente por haberte
ofendido, Dios mío, que eres todo bueno y
mereces todo mi amor. Firmemente prometo,
con el auxilio de tu gracia, confesar mis pecados,
hacer penitencia y enmendar mi vida. Amén.

Prayers

Jesus Prayer

Lord Jesus Christ, Son of God,
have mercy on me, a sinner.

Oración a Jesús

Señor Dios, Hijo de Dios vivo,
ten piedad de mí, este pobre pecador.

I Confess/*Confiteor*

I confess to almighty God
and to you, my brothers and sisters,
that I have greatly sinned,
in my thoughts and in my words,
in what I have done and in what I have
failed to do,

Gently strike your chest with a closed fist.

through my fault, through my fault,
through my most grievous fault;

Continue:

therefore I ask blessed Mary ever-Virgin,
all the Angels and Saints,
and you, my brothers and sisters,
to pray for me to the Lord our God.

Yo Confieso/*Confíteor*

Yo confieso ante Dios todopoderoso
y ante vosotros, hermanos,
que he pecado mucho
de pensamiento, palabra, obra y omisión.

Golpeándose el pecho, dicen:

Por mi culpa, por mi culpa, por mi gran culpa.

Luego prosiguen:

Por eso ruego a santa María, siempre Virgen,
a los ángeles, a los santos
y a vosotros, hermanos,
que intercedáis por mí ante Dios,
nuestro Señor.

Prayer to the Holy Spirit

Come, Holy Spirit, fill the hearts of your faithful.
And kindle in them the fire of your love.
Send forth your Spirit and they shall be created.
And you will renew the face of the earth.
Let us pray.
Lord, by the light of the Holy Spirit you have
taught the hearts of your faithful. In the same
Spirit help us to relish what is right and always
rejoice in your consolation.
We ask this through Christ our Lord. Amen.

Invocación al Espíritu Santo

Ven, Espíritu Santo, llena los corazones de tus
fieles,
y enciende en ellos el fuego de tu amor.
Envía tu Espíritu y serán creadas todas las cosas
y renovarás la faz de la tierra.
Oremos:
¡Oh Dios, que has instruido
los corazones de tus fieles
con luz del Espíritu Santo!,
concédenos que sintamos rectamente
con el mismo Espíritu
y gocemos siempre
de su divino consuelo.
Por Jesucristo Nuestro Señor. Amén.

Prayer of Saint Francis of Assisi

Lord, make me an instrument of your peace:
where there is hatred, let me sow love;
where there is injury, pardon;
where there is doubt, faith;
where there is despair, hope;
where there is darkness, light;
where there is sadness, joy.

O divine Master, grant that I may not so
  much seek
to be consoled as to console,
to be understood as to understand,
to be loved as to love.

For it is in giving that we receive,
it is in pardoning that we are pardoned,
it is in dying that we are born to eternal life.

Oración de San Francisco

Señor, hazme un instrumento de tu paz:
donde haya odio, siembre yo amor;
donde haya injuria, perdón;
donde haya duda, fe en ti;
donde haya tristeza, alegría;
donde haya desaliento, esperanza;
donde haya oscuridad, tu luz.

Maestro, ayúdame a nunca buscar:
el ser consolado, sino consolar;
ser entendido, sino entender;
ser amado, sino amar.
Porque dando es que recibimos,
perdonando es que tú
nos perdonas,
y muriendo es que
volvemos a nacer.

GLOSSARY

Beatitudes teachings of Jesus that show the way to true happiness and tell how to live in God's Kingdom now and always **(35)**

Body of Christ a name for the Church of which Christ is the head. All the baptized are members of the Body. **(61)**

Church the community of baptized people who believe in God and follow Jesus, the Son of God **(11)**

confession telling your sins to the priest **(54)**

conscience an ability given to us by God that helps us make choices about right and wrong. This gift helps us desire to do good and know what God wants us to do. **(35)**

contrition being sorry for your sins and wanting to live better **(45)**

conversion the continual process of becoming the people God made us to be. It is a response to God's love and forgiveness and a turning away from sin. **(53)**

covenant a sacred promise or agreement between God and humans **(24)**

free will the God-given freedom and ability to make choices. God created us with free will so we can have the freedom to choose good. **(15)**

grace God's free and loving gift to humans of his own life and help **(24)**

Holy Trinity the one God in three Divine Persons—God the Father, God the Son, and God the Holy Spirit **(11)**

Kingdom of God the world of love, peace, and justice that is in heaven and is still being built on Earth **(51)**

mercy kindness and concern for those who have wronged us or are suffering. God has mercy on us even though we are sinners. He calls us to show mercy and forgive others as he forgives us. **(24)**

mortal sin a serious sin that causes a person's relationship with God to be broken **(54)**

mystery a spiritual truth that can't be known unless God reveals it, or makes it known to us **(13)**

Original Sin the first sin, committed by Adam and Eve, and then passed down to all human beings after them **(22)**

Paschal Mystery the mystery of Jesus' suffering, Death, Resurrection, and Ascension **(23)**

penance a prayer or an action to help us repair the harm caused by our sins **(55)**

Prayer of Absolution words spoken by the priest during the Sacrament of Penance and Reconciliation to grant forgiveness of sins in God's name **(64)**

reconcile to be reunited or restored to friendship or relationship **(25)**

Seven Sacraments special signs and celebrations that Jesus gave his Church. They allow us to share in God's life and work. **(25)**

sin a person's choice to disobey God on purpose and do what he or she knows is wrong. Sins hurt our relationship with God and other people. **(15)**

temptation wanting to do something we should not, or not wanting to do something we should. It is not a sin, but can lead a person to sin. So we need to avoid temptations to sin. **(25)**

Ten Commandments God's laws that tell people how to love him and others **(34)**

venial sin a sin that hurts a person's friendship with God but does not completely break it **(54)**

Works of Mercy actions that show care for the physical and spiritual needs of others **(55)**

Go to **sacraments.osv.com** for multimedia glossary and interactive review.

Acknowledgments:

Excerpts from the English translation of *Rite of Baptism for Children* © 1969, International Commission on English in the Liturgy Corporation (ICEL); excerpts from the English translation of *Rite of Penance* © 1974, ICEL; excerpts from the English translation of *The Roman Missal* © 2010, ICEL. All rights reserved.

Extractos del *Misal Romano* © 1975, Obra Nacional de la Buena Prensa (ONBP) y Conferencia del Episcopado Mexicano (CEM). Extractos del *Ritual de la Penitencia*, Tercera Edición © 2003, ONBP y CEM.

Scripture selections taken from the *New American Bible*, revised edition © 2010, 1991, 1986, 1970 by the Confraternity of Christian Doctrine, Washington, D.C., and are used by license of the copyright owner. All rights reserved. No part of the *New American Bible* may be reproduced in any form without permission in writing from the copyright owner.

Excerpts from the English translation of the *Catechism of the Catholic Church* for the United States of America copyright © 1994, United States Catholic Conference, Inc.—Libreria Editrice Vaticana. English translation of the *Catechism of the Catholic Church: Modifications from the Editio Typica* copyright © 1997, United States Catholic Conference, Inc.—Libreria Editrice Vaticana. Used by permission. All rights reserved.

Los pasajes de la traducción española del *Catecismo Católico de los Estados Unidos para Adultos* © 2007 Libreria Editrice Vaticana. Todos los derechos reservados. El licenciatario exclusivo en los Estados Unidos es la Conferencia de Obispos Católicos de los Estados Unidos, Washington, D.C. y todas las solicitudes del *Catecismo Católico de los Estados Unidos para Adultos* deben ser dirigidas a la Conferencia de Obispos Católicos de los Estados Unidos.

Quotations from papal and other Vatican documents are from www.vatican.va and copyright © Libreria Editrice Vaticana.

"Peace Prayer" from *Catholic Household Blessings and Prayers Revised Edition*. Translation copyright © 2007 by United States Conference of Catholic Bishops.

"Un Acto de Contrición" del *Libro católico de oraciones* © 1984, de Catholic Book Publishing Corp.

"Oración de San Francisco" de *Oraciones Católicas del Pueblo de Dios* © 2003 de Arquidiócesis de Chicago: Liturgy Training Publications.

Meet Jesus

How do you get to know someone?

Most of the time we start by learning his or her name. As we spend time with our new friend, we discover more about this person.

It's something like that with Jesus. Jesus has many titles. In the Bible, we read that he called himself by different names. This helps us understand more about him, his Father, and the Holy Spirit. We discover what it means to be his friends and live as his disciples.

This book has introduced you to six important titles or names of Jesus. Place the sticker with the correct title next to each picture and description of Jesus.

Place sticker here

The Holy Trinity is one God in three Divine Persons—God the Father, God the Son, and God the Holy Spirit. Jesus is the Second Person of the Holy Trinity.

Place sticker here

God the Father sent Jesus to save us from sin and death.

Place sticker here

Jesus healed people's bodies and souls by his divine power as the Son of God.

Place sticker here

Jesus is the King of our hearts and lives. He welcomes all people to turn away from sin and enter into God's Kingdom.

Place sticker here

Sometimes we get lost because we turn away from God's love. But Jesus, the Good Shepherd, will never give up on helping us return to his Father's love.

Place sticker here

We are joined to Jesus and all those who have faith in him as members of his Body, the Church.

Entering the Mystery

The Paschal Mystery is the suffering, Death, Resurrection, and Ascension of Jesus. Because of the Paschal Mystery, we have the chance to live forever with God.

In Baptism, the Holy Spirit unites us to Jesus. We die to our old lives and rise to a new life in Jesus. We enter into Jesus' Paschal Mystery. Every Sacrament celebrates and draws us into Christ's Paschal Mystery.

Place the stickers that show the parts of Jesus' Paschal Mystery around the cross.

Suffering

Death

Place sticker here

Place sticker here

Place sticker here

Place sticker here

Resurrection

Ascension

Parts of the Sacrament

In Penance and Reconciliation, we die to sin and rise to new life through God's forgiveness.

Place the correct part of the Sacrament sticker next to its description below. For help, look back through your book!

Place sticker here	We are sorry for the sins we have committed and will try really hard not to repeat them.
Place sticker here	We confess our sins to the priest.
Place sticker here	The priest gives us prayers to say or actions to do to help us show that we are truly sorry for our sins. This helps us to repair the harm we've caused and be more loving, like Jesus.
Place sticker here	The priest absolves us and forgives us in Jesus' name for our sins. We receive God's mercy and are restored to a life of grace.

Penance

CONFESSION

Second Person *of the* Trinity

The Good **SHEPHERD**

ACT OF **CONTRITION**

CHRIST *the* **KING**

the **HEALER**

The SAVIOR

CONTRITION

Jesus *and* His Body *the* Church

RECONCILIATION ROOM

Absolution

Check out the maze on the outside of your book. It begins with a star. At the end of the maze, Jesus waits for you with wide-open arms. Draw yourself at the beginning of the maze. Then find your way to Jesus. Be careful, though! Watch out for wrong turns.

When you get to a place where you have to decide which way to go, write the letters HS. This reminds you to listen for the Holy Spirit's guidance. When you have decisions to make, remember to pray, "Holy Spirit, help me to know and do what Jesus asks of me."

Some of the paths might take more energy and more courage. You can always count on the Holy Spirit to help you find your way to Jesus.

Our Sunday Visitor
sacraments.osv.com

ISBN: 978-1-61278-462-5
Item Number: CU542